W9-BMT-857

NOTORIOUS AMERICANS AND THEIR TIMES

Al CAPONE
and the Roaring Twenties

by

DAVID C. KING

Consulting Editor
ROBERT JOHNSTON
Yale University

BLACKBIRCH PRESS, INC.
WOODBRIDGE, CONNECTICUT

Published by Blackbirch Press, Inc.
260 Amity Road
Woodbridge, CT 06525

e-mail: staff@blackbirch.com
Web site: www.blackbirch.com

©1999 by Blackbirch Press, Inc.

Acknowledgment
The publisher would like to
thank Paul W. Heimel, author
of *Eliot Ness: The Real Story*,
for his expert advice.

Printed in the United States

10 9 8 7 6 5 4 3 2

Library of Congress Cataloging-in-Publication Data
King, David C.
Al Capone and the roaring twenties / by David C. King.
    p.   cm. — (Notorious Americans and their times)
   Includes bibliographical references and index.
   Summary: The story of one of America's most infamous and power-
ful gangsters set in Prohibition Chicago during the nineteen twenties.
   ISBN 1-56711-218-8 (lib. bdg.)
   1. Capone, Al, 1899–1947—Juvenile literature. 2. Criminals—
Illinois—Chicago—Biography—Juvenile literature. 3. Organized crime—
Illinois—Chicago—History—Juvenile literature. 4. Prohibition—
Illinois—Chicago—Juvenile literature. 5. Nineteen twenties—Juvenile
literature. 6. United States—History—1919–1933—Juvenile literature.
[1.Capone, Al, 1899–1947. 2. Criminals. 3. Organized crime. 4. Prohibition. 5. United States—History—1919–1933.] I. Title. II. Series.
HV6248.C17K56   1999
364.1'092—dc21   98-14591
[b]   CIP
                                           AC

Table of Contents

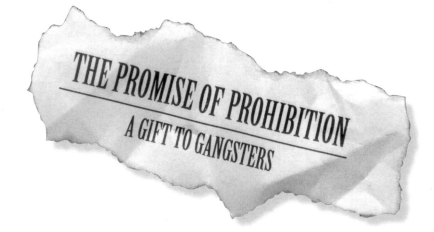

Chapter 1

THE PROMISE OF PROHIBITION
A GIFT TO GANGSTERS

*I*n 1920, America's prospects for the decade ahead did not look promising. The nation was in an economic depression—a time when many businesses fail. Thousands of industrial workers were on strike to demand higher wages and a shorter work week. Adding to Americans' sense of uneasiness was their fear of Communist revolutionaries from Russia. Many thought these revolutionaries were entering the country and contributing to industrial workers' unhappiness. (Communists believed that businesses should be owned by the government, and the profits should be shared by all.)

By the end of the decade, many Americans were worse off than they were at the beginning. In 1929, the stock market crashed. Within a year, the nation was plunged into the Great Depression, which was far more serious than the depression of 1920.

Opposite: *A man waits to enter a speakeasy. From inside, a guard peers through the peephole to make sure there are no Prohibition agents.*

Between the beginning and the end of the decade, however, was one of the wildest, craziest, and most prosperous periods in America's history. The economy grew as never before. People suddenly had more money and more leisure time. And booming businesses provided them with new ways to spend their time and money. Dozens of inventions promised to make life easier, or more fun, or both. This was an age of fast cars, sports heroes, movie stars, daring aviators, stock-market millionaires, and big-time gangsters. It is no wonder that this decade has been nicknamed the "Roaring Twenties."

The 1920s "roared" despite the nation's harsh Prohibition law, which outlawed alcoholic beverages. Prohibition opened the door for gangsters to operate on a grand scale. They could quietly sell the outlawed liquor and make huge profits. One very successful gangster who became famous for his power, charm, and violent ways was Al "Scarface" Capone.

The Gangster's Apprentice

Alphonse Capone grew up in an Italian neighborhood in Brooklyn, New York. Born on January 17, 1899, he was the fourth son of an Italian couple. They had come to America from Naples, Italy, six years earlier. Al's parents were part of the great wave of European immigrants who made up one third of New York City's population at the turn of the century. By then, there were more Italians in New York City than in some of the larger cities in Italy.

Young Al lost interest in school by the time he was in sixth grade, so most of his education took place on the tough, crowded streets bordering the Brooklyn Navy Yard. He grew up fast and big. Al had a heavy, muscular build and large, beefy hands, like a prizefighter's. And because of his fiery temper, he used his fists often.

By age 11, Al belonged to a kids' gang on Manhattan's tough Lower East Side. Four years later, he joined an adult gang called the "Five Points Gang." Their major illegal business was selling so-called "protection" to shop owners. This protection, which supposedly allowed shop owners to conduct their business undisturbed, turned out to be protection from the gang members themselves.

Al was not too young to be noticed and remembered by the head of the gang, Johnny Torrio. He was a small, sharply dressed man who relied on others to supply the "muscle" when he needed it. He was on the rise in the criminal world, and he was called to Chicago to work for a big-time crook there. Al stayed in New York and went to work for one of Torrio's pals, Frankie Yale. (His real name was Francesco Ioele.)

Yale had made a lot of money through extortion (the threat of force to get someone to cooperate). He used the money to open a pair of nightclubs on Coney Island, in South Brooklyn. He also branched out into other businesses—owning racehorses, backing prizefighters, and even producing his own line of cigars. All of Yale's commercial ventures thrived because they relied on the terror of extortion. Anyone who refused to sell him a racehorse or stock a store's shelves with Yale cigars would be beaten.

While he was working as a bartender for Yale at the age of 18, Al's explosive temper led to a fight with a customer. The customer slashed Al's face with a knife, leaving him with a long scar. And that's how Al got his lifelong nickname—"Scarface."

When he was 19, Capone married Mary "Mae" Coughlin, the daughter of Irish immigrants. Their only child, Al "Sonny," Jr., was born shortly before the wedding. Al remained devoted to his son throughout his criminal career, but marriage did nothing to calm his temper. Soon after he married, he was in a fight with a member of another gang. Al's powerful fists nearly killed

A player for the Chicago Cubs autographs a ball for Sonny while Capone looks on.

him, and the man's gang swore revenge. In order to get Al safely out of town, Frankie Yale sent him to Capone's old boss, Johnny Torrio, who was in Chicago.

Al Capone and his family arrived in Chicago in December 1919. The timing was perfect for him and for Torrio. The Eighteenth Amendment to the Constitution, which established the law of Prohibition, was about to go into effect. Johnny Torrio had big ideas for a city and a nation that was quickly going "dry" (without alcohol).

The Prohibition Movement

More than a century before the Prohibition Amendment became law, Thomas Jefferson had urged Americans to plant vineyards. He hoped that wines, with their low alcohol content, might replace rum, whiskey, and other strong liquors that Americans consumed in large quantities. By 1830, Americans drank seven gallons of hard liquor per person in a year—twice as much as Americans drink on average today.

In the mid-1800s, a reform movement (called the temperance movement) appealed to Americans to become more temperate—more moderate in their drinking. After 1870, women took the lead in this movement, forming two powerful organizations: the Woman's Christian Temperance Union (WCTU) and, in 1895, the Anti-Saloon League of America (ASL). Temperance reformers thought that saloons, and the drunkenness they encouraged, were a result of the new urban-industrial age that was taking shape. America was changing from a largely rural and agricultural nation to one of factories and fast-growing cities. The reformers viewed cities as places of sin and temptation, places that lured young Americans away from traditional values of thrift and hard work. A typical anti-saloon booklet warned that "in this age of cities… temptations to our youth increase, such as foul [motion] pictures…gambling slot machines, saloons, and Sabbath breaking…. We are trying to raise saints in hell." To some women, the saloons represented a threat to their home lives. Husbands who got drunk in saloons were more likely to hit their wives and children. These men also wasted family income.

Carrie Nation's "hatchetation" attacks on Kansas saloons made her famous.

One of the most radical members of the WCTU was Carrie Nation, who took direct action against saloons in her native state of Kansas. With a hatchet in hand, she destroyed liquor bottles and furniture. Her "hatchetation" technique earned her some favorable publicity, but it also got her arrested!

In the 1880s, the temperance movement became part of a much larger social reform movement to end political corruption, help those living in poverty, and win voting rights for women (referred to as woman suffrage). Under the leadership of Carrie Chapman Catt, among others, this movement involved women at the local and state level. The leaders did not pressure Congress to allow women to vote. Instead, the reformers brought the voting rights issue to the attention of those who were working for state-wide bans on the sale of alcoholic beverages.

The two campaigns—woman suffrage and Prohibition—made progress together. By 1917, women had won the right to vote in 15 states, and 21 states had passed anti-saloon laws.

In 1917, when the United States entered World War I (1914–1918), both Prohibition and woman suffrage became patriotic issues. Prohibition reformers, for example, could point out the dangers alcohol posed for workers in defense industries or soldiers in the trenches. In addition, they argued, alcohol required

Many women who marched for the right to vote also supported the temperance movement.

millions of tons of grain that should be used to feed soldiers and workers. And voting rights leaders pointed out that if women could drive ambulances and work in vital defense plants, they certainly should have the right to vote.

In December 1917, Congress passed the Eighteenth Amendment to the Constitution, creating a nationwide ban on the "manufacture, sale, or transportation of intoxicating liquors." The amendment was ratified (approved) by the states in 1919. The Volstead Act, which described how Prohibition would be enforced, went into effect in January 1920. Congress passed the Nineteenth Amendment giving women the right to vote in June 1919. It was ratified the next year, in time for women to vote in the 1920 presidential election.

The Desire for "Normalcy"

Prohibition was one way Americans responded to an age of change and uncertainty. The nation in 1920 seemed to be caught between two worlds. The world that seemed to be slipping away was one of small farms and stable villages, of closely knit families and a stern morality. It seemed as if that world was being replaced by horizons of smoke-belching factories and crowded, crime-ridden streets. The 1920 U.S. Census (the official count of all the people in the country) showed that, for the first time, more Americans lived in cities and large towns than in rural areas.

The horrors of World War I added to people's feelings of anxiety and uncertainty. American soldiers had marched off to war in 1917 with bands playing, flags waving, and crowds cheering. The entire nation was caught up in the patriotic spirit of the moment. This was to be, in the words of President Woodrow Wilson, "the war to make the world safe for democracy." He had convinced the nation that they were participating in a great moral crusade. But on the battlefield, Americans were horrified by the death and destruction produced by the world's first modern war. When the veterans returned home, they wanted to turn their backs on Europe. They refused to listen to Wilson's urgent plea that the United States should join the League of Nations in order to avoid future wars. Instead, Americans chose isolation rather than international involvement.

The nation's fear of communism encouraged this tendency toward isolation. The Communists had taken control in Russia, and Communist revolutions spread throughout much of Europe. When a series of strikes swept across the United States in 1919, many saw it as the work of Communists. (Americans referred to them as "Reds" because the Russian flag was red.) When no revolution developed and labor difficulties died down, the "Red Scare," as this exaggerated fear of communism was called, gradually melted away in 1920. But it left many Americans with a deep distrust of outsiders.

In the presidential election of 1920, the Republican candidate, Senator Warren G. Harding, said exactly the right thing to ease people's anxiety. "America's present need," he declared, "is not heroics, but healing; not nostrums [cure-alls], but normalcy; not revolution, but restoration; not agitation, but adjustment; not surgery, but serenity." Harding's message, combined with his pleasant good looks and friendly, small-town personality, swept him and the Republican party into office.

The election gave Americans the hope that post-war life would see a return to "normalcy"—a word invented by Harding. In a similar way, people began the Prohibition Era with a sense that it could somehow lead to a better America and a return to long-cherished values. As an Anti-Saloon League pamphlet announced, "Now for an era of clear thinking and clean living."

Speakeasies and Bootleggers

While the Eighteenth Amendment ended the legal manufacture and sale of beer, wine, and liquor, it did nothing to reduce Americans' thirst for these beverages. In addition, Congress had authorized only 1,600 agents to enforce Prohibition laws. People quickly found ways to get around the new restrictions. Some resorted to "bathtub gin"—homemade creations that were sometimes dangerous enough to kill or blind a person. But most people who wanted liquor visited a speakeasy—a private club or business with an illegal bar. In New York City, Prohibition forced the closing of 15,000 bars in operation before the law went into effect. They were replaced by an estimated 32,000 speakeasies!

Liquor, wine, and beer were supplied by people called "bootleggers." The term dated back to the early 1900s, when smugglers hid bottles of liquor in their boots, carrying the liquor into states where it was already illegal. During Prohibition, smugglers used yachts and fishing boats to sail outside U.S. territorial waters, where waiting ships supplied them with cases of liquor produced in other parts of the world. Illegal breweries and distilleries also operated within the nation's borders. (Breweries make beer, and distilleries make liquor.) They were usually disguised as some other legal business. In every city, rival gangs battled over territory and stole each other's truckloads of beer, wine, and liquor.

Torrio's Chicago Gangland

In Chicago, Johnny Torrio wanted to go into bootlegging on a large scale, but his boss, "Big Jim" Colosimo, was against it. Colosimo had made a fortune from gambling, and he wanted to settle into a respectable life as a restaurant owner. Early in 1920, Colosimo was shot and killed as he left his office, probably by Frankie Yale, brought in as the "hit man." The man who

Police raid one of the many illegal breweries that flourished during Prohibition.

benefitted from Colosimo's death was Johnny Torrio, who took control of Big Jim's empire.

Torrio had a special genius for organization, and he quickly organized Colosimo's territory for the distribution of liquor, wine, and beer. Beer accounted for more than 90 percent of illegal Prohibition profits. Torrio made a deal with breweries that were still licensed to sell "near-beer," which was beer with a low alcohol content of less than 0.5 percent. The near-beer business was a perfect cover for producing as much regular beer as Torrio's gang could sell.

Most of the 1,600 agents hired to enforce Prohibition laws were not very successful at their work. Poorly trained and underpaid, some found it easier to cooperate with bootleggers and speakeasy owners. Two remarkable exceptions were Isadore Einstein and Moe Smith, a pair of plump men who became known as Izzy and Moe.

Izzy and Moe became masters of disguise and trickery in order to get past the guards who protected the speakeasies. Sometimes Izzy would pound on the door and shout, "How about a drink for a tired Prohibition agent?" Since he did not look like a law enforcement officer, he usually gained admittance. On other occasions, the pair carried musical instruments and walked in with a band hired for the evening. Once they were served their drinks, Izzy and Moe had evidence to back up an arrest. In his jacket pocket, each man had a small funnel, with a rubber tube connecting it to a hidden flask. Most of the drink went into the flask, to be produced in court.

Over a period of five years, Izzy and Moe made 4,392 arrests. More than 90 percent of these arrests led to convictions. This was a remarkable record. The trouble was that Izzy and Moe were funny, and the newspaper stories of their adventures were highly entertaining. The two men even invited reporters along on some of their raids. Their superiors frowned on this kind of publicity and, late in 1925, they were dismissed "for the good of the service." An official explained, "This service must be dignified. Izzy and Moe belong on the vaudeville stage." The two pals went into the insurance business instead, and did well.

Izzy and Moe raid a distillery, which manufactured phoney labels in addition to liquor.

Torrio still needed muscle to keep other gangs from moving into his territory and to persuade even the smallest speakeasies to buy only from him. Al Capone was willing to do anything Torrio asked of him and he worked hard to learn from his boss. Capone also showed his initiative by disguising his band of gunmen as a second-hand furniture business. Torrio trained Capone in using techniques of persuasion, rather than always acting like a thug. He even made Capone attend night school to polish his speech and manners. Within a year of his arrival, 21-year-old Al Capone was Torrio's right-hand man.

Torrio's most clever idea was to organize the leaders of all of Chicago's gangs. He persuaded them to divide the city and suburbs into territories. Each gang respected the boundaries of the others. The gangs obtained liquor, wine, and beer from any source they chose, or bought it at a fair price from Torrio. And most important, Torrio used his personal contacts, established by Colosimo, and a lot of bribery money to make sure that neither the police nor politicians interfered with anyone's business. Torrio and others paid more than a million dollars to police officers and city officials to keep them from cracking down on the gangs' operations. The outlaws also contributed huge sums to the election campaigns of some Chicago politicians—including the mayor.

From 1920 on, the gangs enjoyed more than three years of relative peace and illegal prosperity. Business expanded so much and so fast that Torrio soon had Capone buying vehicles for their own trucking company. Prohibition seemed to make it possible for gangsters to succeed, not by stealing from people, but by providing them with the alcoholic beverages they wanted.

Chapter 2

The hard times that followed World War I did not last long. Factories adjusted to the slower pace of peacetime production. And after years of wartime shortages, consumers were eager to buy again. President Harding and Congress cut taxes on business profits and on the incomes of the wealthy. They hoped business leaders and Americans who were financially well off would invest more money in the economy. By late 1921, the economy was beginning to boom again. The Republicans took the credit for this development, and for the rest of the decade, their party called itself the "party of prosperity."

The twenties did not bring the return to "normalcy" that Harding promised, however. It was a decade of great change as well as prosperity. Much of this change was brought on by Henry Ford's Model T and the automobile revolution that it created.

Crime as Big Business

In Chicago, Johnny Torrio had
decided to make his bootlegging
operation look more respectable.
He and Al Capone opened hotels
and established business-like
offices. Rivalries among the
gangs were still troublesome,
though. When things got out of
control, Capone was told never
to kill gang leaders. Instead,
he would send a "message" by
beating or killing one or two
of a gang's hired thugs.

Johnny Torrio

Torrio protected the gangs by
using his influence in government and in the courts. He
made sure that any gang
member arrested for a crime—even murder—would either not
stand trial or would be acquitted (found innocent). Capone bribed
witnesses to lie to protect the accused. He reminded jurors that
a "not guilty" vote was like health insurance for themselves and
their families. A "guilty" vote, on the other hand, could bring
painful revenge. Gangsters themselves followed their own pecu-
liar code of honor. They would never "rap" (identify) another
crook, even one who committed a crime against them.

The election of a reform-minded mayor in Chicago caused
Torrio and Capone more headaches than troublesome gang leaders
did. Police began raiding speakeasies and breweries, smashing
equipment, and locking the doors for as much as a year. Torrio
himself had to pay a $2,500 fine for bootlegging. The city's more

strict enforcement of the Prohibition law convinced Torrio and Capone to move their headquarters close to, but outside of, Chicago's city limits. They chose Cicero, the fifth-largest city in Illinois, for a new base.

In 1923, Torrio took a long vacation in Italy, and he left the move to Cicero in Capone's hands. Capone established the crime organization's headquarters in a hotel, where steel shutters protected the windows. He also opened the Hawthorne Smoke Shop as a front (disguise) for gambling operations. In addition, Torrio's organization continued to supply alcoholic beverages to the speakeasies in its Chicago territory. Capone, Torrio, and their supporters were enjoying the benefits of the nation's new prosperity.

The Automobile Revolution

The development and production of automobiles contributed to this widespread prosperity and changed the way Americans lived. The man most responsible for the automobile revolution was an engineer from Detroit named Henry Ford.

In the early 1900s, automobiles were expensive, mostly used as toys for the rich. Early models were also hard to start and difficult to refuel. Since most cars had no roofs, passengers were exposed to the weather—good or bad. A reliable, inexpensive vehicle was needed, and Henry Ford led the way in building a good car that people could afford.

Ford was guided by a simple theory: "Mass production," he said, "precedes mass consumption and makes it possible by reducing costs." By producing many automobiles at once, he would lower his costs. As a result, more people could afford to buy his cars. He achieved his goals by introducing assembly-line production. Traditionally, workers gathered together all the

automobile parts and then assembled a vehicle. Ford brought
the parts to the worker. Each worker stayed in one place, while
a conveyor belt brought him the parts he needed to do his job.
After a worker finished his operations, the conveyor belt moved
the parts on to the next person, who did another task. Assembly-
line work was boring, but it was amazingly efficient. Instead
of taking 12 hours to assemble a car, Ford's workers eventually
lowered the time to one car every 1½ hours!

The first Ford Model Ts—the only model Ford produced for
20 years—sold for about $900 in 1908. This was less than half
the price of other automobiles. As production increased, prices
were lowered even more. By 1924, a Model T cost only $290.
Between 1908 and 1926, Ford Motor Company sold 15 million

Henry Ford's Model T was the first mass-produced car in the United States.

of them. One out of every five cars on the road was a Model T, which motorists affectionately called "Tin Lizzies."

As other companies copied Ford's assembly-line techniques, the manufacture of automobiles became the nation's leading industry. Competitors began to edge ahead of Ford by changing models each year and offering customers a range of colors. Ford stubbornly stuck to the Model T and scorned colors. He told his customers, "[Buy a Model T] in any color you choose so long as it's black." Competition finally forced Ford to introduce his next model, the Model A, in a range of colors.

People would always remember that it was Ford who had "put America on wheels." Humorist Will Rogers said, "Good luck, Mr. Ford. It will take 100 years to tell whether you have helped us or hurt us. But you certainly didn't leave us like you found us."

As automobile production increased, old dirt roads were replaced by more than 100,000 miles of paved highways. Repair garages and filling stations multiplied on the nation's roads, and so did restaurants, motels (called "tourist homes"), and trailer parks. Workers were needed for all of these new or expanding businesses.

Changing the Face of American Business

Henry Ford's business practices were almost as revolutionary as his production methods. In 1914, he stunned the business world by suddenly doubling his workers' wages and reducing their workdays to eight hours. He reasoned that if the workers had more money and more time, they would buy more cars— hopefully Fords. He also permitted car dealers to sell on credit, which means the dealers allowed customers to pay for their cars gradually, over a period of time. For as little as $25 for a down payment (a first payment), a family could drive off in a brand new Model T. By the mid-1920s, three out of four vehicles were bought on credit. Buying on credit became common when people wanted other large items, too, such as furniture.

Widespread advertising added to the growth in consumer spending. Companies and banks that had spent little on advertising a decade earlier were now spending up to $100 million a year on ads. Between 40 and 75 percent of every newspaper was devoted to advertising. Billboards multiplied along the nation's highways. The billboards were one of the most effective ways of reaching a national audience. One corporation paid $140,000 per month to blanket the country's roads with 17,000 signs.

The automobile produced another new development. It enabled city workers to move to the suburbs and commute

⌐ THE FLORIDA LAND FRENZY ⌐

The Florida land boom reflected the dizzying atmosphere of the decade. It came about partly because the automobile made it easier and more fun to travel long distances. Around 1920, American motorists became interested in Florida. Cars, trucks, and buses began to crowd the Dixie Highway. Visitors started to buy building lots in the land of sunshine and beaches. The lots sold at bargain prices, and soon many people were speculating on Florida real estate. They bought land with the hope that it would soon be much more valuable. Then they would sell it. A lot purchased for $500 might be sold three months later for ten times that amount.

Newspapers carried stories of small fortunes made in an incredibly short time. One journalist decided to test the real estate fever by purchasing land she had never seen for $2,500. She sold it less than six months later for $35,000. Some people bought lots that they later learned were in quarry pits or in swamps. But it hardly mattered because someone else would come along and pay more for it! As one real estate salesman said, "The people who have made real fortunes check their brains before leaving home. Buy anything. You can't lose." During the years of the land boom, more than 3 million people made the trip to Florida each year, investing hundreds of millions of dollars.

The Florida land boom ended quite suddenly. By early 1926, more people were selling land than buying it, and prices began to drop. Thousands who borrowed money from banks to buy real estate failed to make their payments. Then, in September 1926, a hurricane ripped through the Florida coast. The boom was over. A few people got rich, but most did not. And several thousand people lost everything.

to work. An explosive growth of the suburbs led to the construction of homes, schools, hospitals, and other buildings. The real estate business was booming.

The Growth of Electrical Power

One of the dazzling options offered in new suburban houses was the "all electric home," which featured the use of electrical power for heating, air-conditioning, and operating various appliances. The creation of electricity for lighting and for powering machinery was still a relatively recent development. New ways of generating electricity enabled power companies to increase production and reduce costs. By 1929, more than three-quarters of the nation's factories were using electrical power, and so were most homes in cities and large towns.

The growth of electrical power and new inventions made possible a dazzling array of products, including radios, vacuum cleaners, electric stoves, refrigerators, and washing machines. With the economy growing, Americans had more money to spend, and they bought these products as fast as manufacturers could turn them out.

Corruption and Scandals

President Harding was an honest politician who chose his advisers badly. He had appointed several outstanding people to important positions, but for advice he turned to a group of old pals from Ohio who held Cabinet positions. Americans referred to them as his "Poker Cabinet." Some of these individuals made use of political office for their own personal benefit. The attorney general, Harry Daugherty, who headed the country's Justice Department, sold legal favors. When rumors of Daugherty's activities began to circulate, his assistant committed suicide.

Another member of the Poker Cabinet, the head of the Veterans' Bureau, received a prison sentence for selling leftover hospital supplies to private companies.

The worst scandal involved Albert B. Fall, the secretary of the Interior Department. He sold U.S. Navy oil reserves (extra supplies) at Elk Hills, California, and Teapot Dome, Wyoming, to two private companies. A Congressional investigation led to Fall's conviction on bribery and other charges. He became the first Cabinet officer in the nation's history to go to prison.

As news of Fall's "Teapot Dome Scandal" emerged, Harding became upset. In the summer of 1923, he decided to make a series of public appearances across the country to win back the nation's confidence. But the strain was too much for him. He collapsed suddenly and died in California on August 2, 1923. Vice President Calvin Coolidge became president.

President Warren G. Harding

Coolidge, who had become famous for his handling of a Boston police strike in 1919, was very honest. As president, though, he was content to do as little as possible. A man of few words, one of his most famous statements was, "The business of America is business." Government agencies that had been established to regulate businesses now went out of their way to help them run more smoothly. As *The Wall Street Journal* put it, "Never before, here or anywhere else, has a government been so completely fused with business." Coolidge was easily elected for a full term in 1924.

Election Time in Cicero

In Cicero, Illinois, Al Capone's first involvement in a political campaign was crude and violent. To make sure that Mayor John Klenha was re-elected in 1924, Capone had carloads of gunmen patrol the streets. Their job was to make sure that voters for the opposition did not reach the polls in time. An outraged judge allowed dozens of Chicago policemen to cross the city limits and enter Cicero in order to stop Capone's men. The police arrived too late to alter the outcome of the election. In a brief gunfight, however, Capone's brother Frank was shot and killed.

Al Capone made sure Mayor John Klenha was re-elected in 1924.

A few weeks later, Mayor Klenha ignored Capone's orders on some issue that interested Capone. The gang leader met the mayor on the city hall steps and knocked him cold. Soon after that incident, Capone had his thugs break up a meeting of the city counsel. They beat one council member and sent the rest home.

After this short period of violence, Capone changed his tactics. Maybe he remembered Johnny Torrio's instructions about taking a business-like approach to their crime operations. Capone decided to win back the mayor's favor by helping him clean up street crime. Robberies and burglaries practically disappeared. By the time Torrio returned from Italy, the organization was running smoothly, and it was earning good profits. Cicero was turning out to be a perfect base of operations.

The interiors of most speakeasies were very plain.

Although the city covered barely 6 square miles, it now had between 120 and 160 speakeasies. Torrio and Capone split their profits in half, and they were becoming wealthy. Government records would later show that gambling alone brought each partner $123,000 in 1924. And gambling was only a sideline to their bootlegging business.

Chapter 3

THE JAZZ AGE
"MUSICAL FIREWORKS"
AND GANGLAND WARS

*T*he ideals of the temperance reformers disappeared in a new age of fast cars, easy money, and widespread spending. Millions of Americans openly disobeyed the Prohibition law by going to speakeasies, where young people found the forbidden atmosphere exciting. Drinking bootleg liquor was a way to rebel against the patriotic mood that had dominated America during World War I. Fiction writer F. Scott Fitzgerald echoed the feelings of many when he wrote:

> *We were tired of Great Causes. Scarcely had the staider [more serious] citizens of the republic caught their breath when the wildest of all generations, which had been adolescent during the confusion of the War, danced into the limelight.... [We] embarked on the greatest, gaudiest spree in history.*

Chicago's Gangland Wars

The peace among Chicago's gangs, arranged by Johnny Torrio and Capone, came to an end in 1924. The first gang leader to make trouble was Charles Dion "Deany" O'Banion, whose gang controlled the city's North Side. O'Banion's hobby was flowers. He bought a flower shop, where he spent much of his time making floral arrangements for the frequent gangland funerals.

In 1924, O'Banion became involved in a feud with the rulers of Chicago's West Side—the six Genna brothers, known as the Terrible Gennas. He accused the Gennas of selling beer in his territory and ordered some of their trucks hijacked. Torrio and Capone tried to settle the argument, and O'Banion seemed to cooperate. He said he was retiring to Colorado and sold his main brewery to Torrio. Just as Torrio arrived to close the deal, however, police raided the brewery. They seized 500 barrels of beer, and arrested 31 bootleggers, including Torrio and O'Banion.

Torrio believed that O'Banion's carelessness led to the raid, and Torrio now faced a jail sentence for his second conviction for bootlegging. He might have forgiven O'Banion in order to maintain peace, but O'Banion continued to challenge the Gennas, insisting that one of them pay him a gambling debt. That was going too far. On November 10, 1924, O'Banion was in his flower shop when three gunmen came in and murdered him. He was given one of gangland's biggest funerals, with Torrio and Capone among the mourners. Police questioned dozens of suspects (people suspected of a crime), including Capone. Although the evidence indicated that Capone hired Frankie Yale and two other men to kill O'Banion, there were no arrests and no convictions.

The O'Banion murder was just the beginning of the gang warfare that rocked Chicago for the rest of the decade. Early in 1925, just before Torrio went on trial for the brewery arrest,

After a gangland shoot-out in Chicago, the victims' bodies are loaded onto a hearse.

Capone's car was shot at by some of O'Banion's men. Although Capone was not in the car and no one was killed, the incident left him shaken. He immediately had a Cadillac car fitted with steel armor and bulletproof glass. Capone now drove a moving fortress that weighed seven tons.

As Torrio had long suspected, once gang leaders became the targets for murder, all attempts to organize the gangs were doomed. It was now clear that not even Johnny Torrio and Al Capone were safe from violence.

The American public reacted to the gangland killings like spectators at a Wild West shoot-out. They eagerly read detailed newspaper accounts accompanied by plenty of photographs. Reports of hijackings and vicious murders seemed to be part of the exciting times in which they lived. Fortunately, most Americans found more peaceful ways to express their rebellion against authority and tradition.

Jazz and a New Generation of Youth

The spirit of the 1920s found expression in a new musical form called "jazz." African-American composers and musicians had already made important contributions to music by creating gospel music, blues, and the more lively and upbeat ragtime. Jazz was an explosive new sound filled with musicians' creative improvisation: Trumpet players, saxophonists, and other soloists made up melodies while they were performing. The music quickly became very popular throughout the nation, and much of the world. Although jazz began in the South, New York's Harlem soon became a center for exciting music. Night spots featured outstanding bands, such as Duke Ellington's; great singers like Bessie Smith; and solo performers, including the trumpet player Louis Armstrong. Classical composer and conductor

Bessie Smith

Leopold Stokowski wrote that "Jazz has come to stay because it is an expression of the times, of the breathless, energetic, super-active times in which we are living."

Jazz, which one enthusiast called "musical fireworks," was the perfect accompaniment for a young generation determined to have a good time. A good time in the Roaring Twenties meant going to a speakeasy to dance all night, drink liquor, and smoke endless cigarettes. Young middle-class women became "flappers." They wore their hair cut short and topped with head-hugging hats. They dressed in "short" (knee-length) dresses, rolled down stockings, and unbuckled galoshes (rubber boots) instead of shoes. Flappers liked to wear many bracelets and long strings of pearl necklaces. In an unprecedented display of "non-lady-like" behavior, they boasted about their drinking ability. Their dates were young men called "sheiks." They imitated the slicked-down hair of the movie star Rudolph Valentino in his famous movie role as *The Sheik*. The sheiks wore bulky raccoon coats, drove expensive, high-powered cars, cheered for their colleges at football games, and carried hip flasks (bottles) of the best liquor.

Young women and men tried to live the life described in Edna St. Vincent Millay's famous little poem:

My candle burns at both ends;
It will not last the night;
But ah, my foes, and oh, my friends,
It gives a lovely light.

"Burning the candle at both ends" has become a common expression. It means doing something pleasurable to such an extreme that it becomes harmful—which is how many people seemed to take their pleasure in the twenties.

A variety of literary forms flourished throughout the 1920s, with novels being the most popular. F. Scott Fitzgerald's fiction set the tone for the decade. His most famous work was *The Great Gatsby*, a novel about a wealthy bootlegger who is unlucky in love. Ernest Hemingway, in *The Sun Also Rises* and other novels, wrote short, brisk sentences to describe the alienation (unfriendly mood) of many Americans after the war.

American theater, which had emphasized light entertainment, began to experiment with serious drama. The most prominent playwright was Eugene O'Neill, who wrote dark tragedies that explored people's hidden motives and feelings.

In New York's Harlem, African American writers produced a rich variety of literary works in what became known as the Harlem Renaissance. In *God's Trombone*, for example, James Weldon Johnson presented a series of sermons in verse form to celebrate African American preachers. Langston Hughes was probably the most popular writer of the movement. Best known for poetry, he also wrote novels,

F. Scott Fitzgerald

stories, plays, and essays. Zora Neale Hurston gained fame for *Mules and Men*, a collection of African American stories, songs, and sayings. Some of her novels, such as *Their Eyes Were Watching God*, are considered classics.

Resistance to Change

While many Americans were caught up in making money and spending it as fast as they could, millions more did not like what was happening. Some were finding that the new age of prosperity was passing them by, and they resented the government's support of big business. Farmers and many factory workers were not living as well as they had before the 1920s.

In the 1924 presidential election, many who were dissatisfied with the Democrats and Republicans pinned their hopes on a third political party, the Progressive party. Wisconsin Senator Robert M. LaFollette was the party's presidential candidate. Although the Progressives made one of the strongest third-party showings in the nation's history, they lost heavily to the Republican candidate, Calvin Coolidge. The Progressive party soon disappeared.

The Revival of the Ku Klux Klan

One organization that attracted some Americans who disliked urban and industrial change was the Ku Klux Klan (KKK). The KKK was originally formed after the Civil War to prevent newly freed slaves from fully participating in American community life. When it was revived in 1915, the new Klan kept its traditional white robes and grand titles for its officials, such as Imperial Wizard, Klaliff, and Exalted Cyclops. The new KKK also kept its old tools of violence—threats, beatings, and murder.

This time, however, the Klan's victims were not only African Americans. The Klan targeted Jews, Catholics, Communists, labor organizers, foreigners, and non-English-speaking immigrants. Through their efficient, business-style organization, the Klan recruited members from all parts of the country. Most came from rural areas. By 1923, the Klan's membership had reached

The Ku Klux Klan parades in Washington, D.C.

an estimated 5 million, and money was pouring into the KKK headquarters in Georgia.

The Klan's appeal to troubled rural Americans was its message, not its violent methods. Dr. Hiram W. Evans, a former dentist, became Imperial Wizard and the Klan's leading spokesperson. In his speeches and writing, Evans addressed the "plain people...the Americans of the old pioneer stock." These were the Americans, he said, who were members of the "Nordic [white] race, which...has given the world almost the whole of modern civilization." According to Evans, the growth of cities and a wave of new immigrants had led to a breakdown in morality. Much of the fault, he declared, lay with "aliens of Eastern and Southern Europe [who were] tearing down the American standard of living." His solution was to keep foreigners out of the United States and make many Americans who were not white or Protestant feel unwelcome in their own country.

The Ku Klux Klan became a powerful force in politics. Klan support helped elect U.S. senators from 10 states and governors in 11 states. Klan members and others who feared foreign influences continually pressured Congress to limit immigration. Congress responded with immigration laws in 1921, 1924, and 1927. The new laws limited the number of people who could come from Southern or Eastern Europe, Africa, or Asia and settle in the United States.

Almost all of the Klan members were Protestants. Among the basic beliefs of the Klan, as stated by Imperial Wizard Evans, was that "Protestantism must be supreme.... Protestantism contains more than religion. It is the expression in religion of the same spirit of independence, self-reliance, and freedom which are the highest achievement of the Nordic race."

The Klan's religious thoughts were compatible with a trend among some Protestants. In 1910, leaders of several Protestant churches published a series of pamphlets called *The Fundamentals*, which presented their members' basic Christian beliefs. One was the absolute truth of the Bible. The "fundamentalists," as conservative Protestants came to be called, were drawn from the same rural population that supported the Klan.

The Scopes Trial

Throughout the 1920s, fundamentalists were very concerned about an issue that related to education. They did not want public schools to teach the theory of evolution introduced by the nineteenth-century scholar, Charles Darwin. He believed that humans evolved from lower life forms, such as apes. His theory contradicted the Biblical story of creation and therefore upset fundamentalists.

The conflict between fundamentalism and evolutionary theory led to a famous trial in Tennessee. A young teacher named John Scopes agreed to test the state's law against teaching evolution in the classroom by defying the law and teaching Darwin's theory. The Scopes trial attracted the attention of hundreds of reporters. Many Americans became involved in emotional debates throughout the steamy summer of 1925. Scopes was found guilty of teaching evolution and was fined $100. The fundamentalists were convinced they had won a great moral victory.

Despite all the efforts by rural Americans to hold onto their traditions, change rolled on through the decade. In fact, from 1925 on, the twenties seemed to get wilder.

Capone Takes Charge

The forces of change were rocking the foundations of the crime organization in Chicago and Cicero. In mid-January 1925, a judge fined Johnny Torrio $5,000 for operating an illegal brewery

Al Capone in 1928

and sentenced him to a nine-month jail term. The judge allowed him ten days to settle his affairs, and that gave the late O'Banion's gang time to strike. On January 24, two gunmen attacked Torrio outside his apartment, shooting him five times with pistol and shotgun blasts.

Torrio survived the assault and, still recovering, eagerly accepted his jail sentence. He had had enough. He called his lawyers and Al Capone to his jail cell and announced, "It's all yours, Al." As soon as he finished his jail term, he and his wife would head for Italy. Torrio turned everything over to Capone, who promised to send him 25 percent of the profits.

Al Capone now ruled the Torrio-Capone empire, but the organization continued to crumble while gang warfare increased. Of the 46 gangland killings in 1925, some involved a new weapon: a submachine gun, also called a Tommy gun. It could fire 1,000 bullets per minute. Capone was the top gang leader, but he would have to cope with other ambitious leaders who were now arming themselves with military weapons.

Chapter 4

AMERICA LOVES HEROES
LINDBERGH, EARHART, AND...CAPONE

$\mathcal{B}$efore the 1920s, America's greatest heroes were often military or political leaders. Now a new and very different generation of heroes emerged. Some were movie stars, and others were athletes. Aviators and business leaders were celebrities, too. And so were gangsters.

The American public read about the adventures of their heroes in newspapers and magazines, which were published in greater numbers than ever before. Fans could also hear their favorite celebrities on the radio. Or they could go to a movie theater and see these famous men and women in newsreels—short movies on current events. In the competition for readers, listeners, and movie-goers, the media began to exaggerate every news event. The excesses of this publicity gave the 1920s still another nickname, the "Age of Ballyhoo" (exaggeration).

Al Capone at the Top

Al Capone was not well-known outside Chicago. When he was involved in a shooting while on a trip to New York, the city's newspapers listed him as "Al Caponi, a bartender." The public learned his name, however, when Chicago's gang wars brought him nationwide attention in 1926.

With Johnny Torrio gone, Capone launched a vicious campaign to protect himself and regain control of Chicago's crime organizations. First, he attacked the Genna brothers. He ordered the murder of several of the gang members, one or two at a time, to avoid attracting too much press attention. Capone rarely had to use a gun himself, and he always had an alibi. By 1926, the remaining Genna gang was in no position to challenge Capone's authority.

Al Capone fishing and enjoying a morning cigar.

The men who took over Deany O'Banion's gang were a more serious threat than the Gennas. That was made clear on September 20, 1926, in a shooting that made headlines across the country. Capone and his bodyguard were eating lunch in a crowded restaurant across the street from his Cicero headquarters. A parade of ten cars drove slowly past the restaurant. As each car passed by, the men in the car opened fire with shotguns and Tommy guns. Then a gunman emerged from the last car and stood in the restaurant doorway, emptying his submachine gun into the interior.

When the first car approached the restaurant, Capone's bodyguard saw the guns and threw his boss to the floor. The other diners dove under the tables as bullets shattered the windows. Miraculously, no one in the restaurant was hurt, although four people in the vicinity were wounded. Police counted several thousand bullet holes in the restaurant, and 35 cars on the street had holes as well.

As a result of the shooting, Capone's name became known throughout the country. Two weeks later, when the new head of O'Banion's gang and his bodyguard were killed by submachine guns, Capone was again mentioned in all the newspapers, this time as a suspect. He enjoyed the publicity, and he became increasingly friendly with reporters. The reporters, in turn, began to refer to him as the "Big Fellow." They publicized the fact that he paid for all the damages and medical bills resulting from the restaurant shooting. Pretending he was innocent of all gangland killings, he told reporters that he was working for peace:

I've begged those fellows to put away their pistols and talk sense. They've all got families, too.... What makes them so crazy to end up on a slab in the morgue, with their mothers' hearts broken...I don't know.

No one was fooled by Capone's act of innocence. The reporters were well aware that he was responsible for more gangland murders than anyone else. But they made him a celebrity because it sold newspapers.

Entertainment as Big Business

During the twenties, the motion picture and radio industries helped create the nation's new generation of heroes and made Americans a nation of spectators. At the turn of the century, viewers had been fascinated by the first motion pictures—short, flickering films shown in crude movie theaters called "nickelodeons." Movies became more popular after 1920, with the introduction of feature-length silent films. The first movie stars rapidly attracted millions of fans. Rudolph Valentino was romantic, and Douglas Fairbanks was the hero of adventure films. Charlie Chaplin reigned as the king of comedy. Among actresses, Mary Pickford was "America's sweetheart." In 1927, *The Jazz Singer* became the first movie with sound. A year later, Walt Disney produced his first Mickey Mouse cartoon, "Steamboat Willie."

The crowded nickelodeons of earlier days were soon replaced by elegant "motion picture palaces." These highly decorated movie houses could seat from 2,000 to 4,500 people or more, and the seats were usually full. In 1928, for example, Chicago's 12 luxury theaters sold a total of 30 million movie tickets.

Radio was the other great media development of the decade. Until 1920, radios were only used for communications between ships and shore stations. In addition, a few hundred amateurs experimented with a primitive form of radio called a "crystal set." The first station to broadcast on a regular basis was KDKA, in Pittsburgh. The free entertainment it offered was an immediate hit. By 1922, more than 500 stations were on the air, and

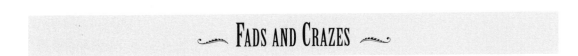

During the twenties, a variety of fads swept the country with lightning speed. This was obvious proof of the power of publicity to influence people's behavior. Fads also showed how swiftly people could be caught up in the excitement of the moment—sometimes with very silly results!

Early in the decade, many people competed with one another to see who could put on the fanciest parties for playing mah-jongg, a Chinese board game. The mah-jongg fad was followed by the crossword-puzzle craze. There were no books of crossword puzzles before 1924. Within a year, there were dozens, and some sold at least 750,000 copies.

Young people who enjoyed dancing the popular Charleston participated in dance contests. Some took part in dance marathons that lasted for a week. One of the silliest fads was flagpole sitting. Alvin "Shipwreck" Kelly drew large crowds by sitting on a tiny platform atop a pole for several days. He didn't dare to sleep for more than several minutes at a time for fear he would tumble to his death. When this craze hit Baltimore, children as young as eight were caught up in it. Avon Freeman, age 15, gained brief fame by perching on a flagpole for ten days. The mayor congratulated him for showing "the pioneer spirit of early America."

Alvin "Shipwreck" Kelly

Americans were spending about $400 million per year on radio equipment. In 1927, when the boxer Gene Tunney defended his heavyweight boxing title against former champ Jack Dempsey, an estimated 40 million people listened to the blow-by-blow radio broadcast from Chicago.

Radio had a widespread impact on American life. Advertisers quickly discovered that radio offered a new way to reach millions of people. The age of the commercial was born, and consumer spending received a tremendous boost. Another result of radio commercials was that brand names began to dominate the market. Americans bought products produced by companies large enough to advertise, sell, and distribute their brands around the nation.

Like the automobile, radio brought rural Americans closer to the mainstream of the nation's life and culture. People in the most remote parts of the country were now listening to the same news, sports, dramas, and comedies as urban Americans.

Larger Than Life Heroes

Radio broadcasts and movie newsreels enabled people to follow the great sports heroes of the day more closely. Rarely has a single decade produced so many outstanding figures. Of all the great athletes, by far the most popular was baseball's George Herman "Babe" Ruth. Ruth's mighty swing, which won him a record 60 homeruns in 1927, filled spectators with awe. So did Ruth's enormous appetite, his love of bootleg beer, and his wild lifestyle.

Writers and radio broadcasters developed an exaggerated and flowery style to excite their audiences about each achievement. When the giant of the tennis world, William "Big Bill" Tilden, won his first U.S. National Championship game, in 1920,

Babe Ruth

The New York Times said the game was "...the most astounding exhibition of tennis, the most nerve-wracking battle that the courts have ever seen."

Swimming also produced towering figures. The most amazing swimming feat of the decade was achieved by 20-year-old Gertrude Ederle. In 1926, she battled heavy seas to become the first woman to swim the English Channel, the 150-mile-wide body of water separating England and France. Ederle beat the men's record by nearly two hours. Sportswriter W.O. McGeehan called it "the greatest sports story in the world."

Of all the stars and heroes of the twenties, none were as wildly celebrated as the aviator Charles A. Lindbergh. On May 21, 1927, he became the first person to fly nonstop across the

Charles A. Lindbergh

In 1921, Amelia Earhart became one of the first women to earn a pilot's license. Over the next decade and a half, she went on to score a series of "firsts." In 1928, as a crew member, she became the first woman to fly across the Atlantic. Four years later, she was the first woman to make a flight alone, setting a new record of less than 15 hours.

Amelia Earhart

Earhart wrote two books and served as vice-president of one of the first passenger airlines. She continued to pursue her flying career, setting a number of records for speed and altitude. In 1937, with Frederick J. Noonan as co-pilot, she attempted an around-the-world flight. On July 2, somewhere over the central Pacific, their twin-engine-plane ran into trouble. The plane's radio went dead, and the efforts of land-based radio operators to make contact with Earhart were met by silence. No trace of the plane or the pilots was ever found. For years, rumors circulated claiming that Earhart was still alive somewhere. Every search proved futile, however. As recently as 1996, parts of a crashed plane that may have been Earhart's were found on a remote Pacific island. But so far, no definite answer has been found to explain how or where Amelia Earhart's plane went down.

Atlantic Ocean from New York to Paris. To the amazement of people around the world, he did it alone, with no navigational equipment other than a compass. Lindbergh landed outside Paris after a flight of 33½ hours. His single-engine plane, the *Spirit of St. Louis*, was nearly torn apart by the 100,000 people who tried to reach their hero.

When the shy, handsome young flier returned to New York City, the harbor was filled with some 400 ships to welcome him. The city gave him a huge ticker-tape parade that has never been equalled. Fans showered him with 1,800 tons of paper ribbons!

Throughout the weeks of wild celebrations that followed his return, Lindbergh remained modest and quiet. For many people, Lindbergh's dignity was as impressive as his flight. He was a refreshing contrast to other heroes created by the media. Journalist Mary B. Mallet explained it this way:

> *We shouted ourselves hoarse. Not because a man had flown across the Atlantic! Not even because he was an American! But because he was as clean in character as he was strong and fine in body; because he put "ethics" above any desire for wealth; because he was as modest as he was courageous; and because—as we now know, beyond any shadow of doubt—these are the things we honor most in life.*

Capone's New Image

By 1927, Capone was playing the part of a celebrity with the help of the media. Reporters found he was quite well informed about a variety of topics, including sports, the government, movies, jazz, and Italian opera. And he liked to talk about them. His favorite subject, however, was Prohibition. He explained to the reporters that he was merely a businessman:

What's Al Capone done then? He's supplied a legitimate demand. Some call it bootlegging.... I call it business. They say I violate the Prohibition law. Who doesn't? They call Al Capone a bootlegger. Yes, it's bootleg while it's on the trucks, but when your host...hands it to you on a silver tray, it's hospitality.

The press and the public were impressed by Capone's success and wealth. He dressed in expensive clothes and wore a gigantic diamond ring. Capone carried a roll of $50,000 in cash, from which he peeled off bills for tips or gifts wherever he went. He gave freely to the poor. At Capone's expense, business owners provided coal, groceries, and clothing to many people in need. As one Cicero police detective said, "My people thought Capone was Robin Hood."

Surrounding Capone was an exciting feeling of danger. He rode in his armored Cadillac, with another car in front and a third behind. When he went for a walk, he required up to 18 bodyguards. When he attended the theater or opera, he bought many seats so he could surround himself with his gang members. Capone also had a network of spies and hired gunmen. In 1927 they saved him from at least ten attempts on his life. This was success gangster style, but it would not last forever.

Chapter 5

**THE DARK SIDE OF THE GOLDEN DECADE
POVERTY AND A MASSACRE**

*D*uring the 1920s, the stock market rose steadily, and some people who bought stocks (shares in a company) made a lot of money. A poem printed in the *Saturday Evening Post* captured people's faith in the stock market, where the "bulls," who bought aggressively, outnumbered the "bears"—the more conservative investors.

> *Oh hush thee, my babe, granny's bought some more shares*
> *Daddy's gone out to play with the bulls and the bears,*
> *Mother's buying on tips and she simply can't lose,*
> *And baby shall have some expensive new shoes!*

The wealth produced on Wall Street, where most stocks were bought and sold, and the great increase in consumer spending helped create the impression that everyone was doing well. But as the popularity of the Ku Klux Klan demonstrated, this was not the case. For millions of Americans, the Golden Twenties were not golden at all.

An Excess of Violence

By 1928, Al Capone realized that he could not control organized crime in Chicago. After several more attempts on his life, he left the region, planning to settle somewhere else. But when Capone entered Los Angeles, New Orleans, and other cities, police immediately escorted him and his bodyguards out of town. City leaders were anxious to avoid the kind of violence that accompanied Al Capone. He finally managed to settle in Florida, where he bought an estate on Palm Island, near Miami Beach. He spent $100,000 on improvements, including the largest swimming pool in the entire state.

Capone felt safe in Florida, but his great empire was beginning to crumble and he soon returned to Chicago to take care of it. Americans were disgusted with the gangland violence, which claimed more than 400 lives during the twenties. As a result of the public's complaints, politicians and police tried to close down speakeasies, distilleries, breweries, and other gang-controlled operations. In New York, Capone's old friend Frankie Yale began hijacking truckloads of liquor scheduled for delivery to Capone's speakeasies and other establishments in Chicago and Cicero. On July 1, 1928, Yale was gunned down on a New York street.

Yale had nearly as many friends as Capone did. There were 104 cars in his funeral procession, with 38 more carrying flowers. Later that year, a total of 15 men connected to Capone were murdered in the space of three months.

Capone struck back on Valentine's Day. His target was an old enemy—George "Bugs" Moran. On February 14, 1929, seven men who worked for Moran were in a Chicago garage preparing trucks to pick up liquor. A Cadillac car pulled up, equipped with a police siren and gong. (The gong was used by police more often than a siren.) Four men got out of the car, two of them in police uniforms. Thinking it was one more nuisance raid, the seven from the Moran gang obeyed the order to line up against the wall. Then the two men who were not in uniforms opened fire, blasting the seven with submachine gun bullets.

The headlines that spread across every front page in the country called the shooting the "St. Valentine's Day Massacre." The event added to the growing public outrage. Even those who

In order to solve the crime, police try to re-create the St. Valentine's Day Massacre—without shooting!

had previously seen something glamorous in underworld life were upset by the crime. Gang violence was spinning out of control. The *Boston Globe* warned that, "There are many reasons to believe that the rest of the United States is growing more like Chicago." Some writers have questioned Capone's connection to the St. Valentine's Day Massacre, largely because he was always careful to have only one or two men killed at a time. But in all probability, Capone was the man behind the massacre. Certainly the authorities and the police were convinced of his guilt.

The St. Valentine's Day Massacre was bound to lead to new pressure on the authorities to do something about gangsters, especially Capone. He would soon feel the law closing in on him—but this time it was not the police, but agents of the Internal Revenue Service.

Poverty in the Land of Plenty

Throughout the 1920s, wages were inching upward. Over 40 percent of the nation's families had annual incomes of more than $2,000. In addition, this was in an age of low prices. Milk cost 11 cents a quart; a dinner at a good restaurant averaged $1.40. An income of $2,000 was enough for a family to live comfortably, and many were making far more than that amount.

More than half of America's families, however, had to get by on less than $2,000 a year. Coal miners and some industrial workers were suffering. But the largest group that was bypassed by the nation's prosperity was made up of farmers and farm workers.

The family-owned farm had been the backbone of the American economy since Colonial days. Even in the middle of the twenties, four out of every ten families still lived on farms or in rural villages. Just a few years earlier, during World War I, the demand for grain had created record profits for farm families. To take advantage of the boom times, they borrowed money from banks to buy or lease more land and to buy the newly developed farm machinery that could increase production.

When the war ended, so did the high prices for grain and other farm products. Agriculture never really recovered. Wheat, for example, had sold for more than $2 a bushel during the war. It was never higher than 67 cents a bushel during the 1920s. While farm income dropped, farmers still had to make payments on the money they had borrowed to buy land and equipment. Many families simply could not keep up. Between 1921 and 1930, more than 400,000 people lost their homes and farms to banks or other creditors (lenders). Many of these families moved to cities. Others became tenant farmers, who paid money to rent the land they farmed, or sharecroppers, who gave landlords a share of the crop as payment.

Many African-American families in the South had lived as sharecroppers since the end of the Civil War. As farm prices declined, thousands abandoned the land and headed for cities in the North and West. During the 1920s, more than 1 million African Americans took part in this great migration. In the cities, they discovered that they sometimes had to live in separate housing, and their children often attended all-black schools. They also experienced job discrimination, and sometimes violence from white people who feared they would lose their jobs to blacks. Despite the obstacles, many African Americans found jobs in such industries as steel, automobiles, and meat packing. More than 70,000 started their own businesses.

Other groups that relied on the land also missed out on the good times. More than 500,000 Mexicans crossed the border into the southwestern United States. While some found city jobs, more than half became migrant farm workers. They moved from farm to farm, living in crude camps and harvesting seasonal crops for pennies a day.

Native Americans also suffered through hard times. Since a law called the Dawes Act was passed in 1887, the government had been attempting to break up the reservations and turn the land over to individual Native American families. Without the support of tribal communities, many of the farms failed. By the mid-1920s, Native Americans had lost 86 million acres—over half the land they had owned in 1887. Thousands escaped rural poverty by moving to the cities, where some became particularly skilled in construction trades. Congress finally granted full citizenship to Native Americans in 1924, but the reversal of the Dawes Act policies did not come until the 1930s.

Isolation and Rootlessness

Many Americans felt isolated and rootless during the 1920s. Fewer people could count on the support of close-knit families and stable communities. Throughout the decade and beyond, millions of people found comfort in fundamentalist religion. There arose a new generation of evangelical preachers who wanted to spread the teachings of Jesus Christ. They used modern business organizational models and advertising techniques to reach huge audiences. Billy Sunday, the most famous of the preachers, drew crowds of 100,000 to his outdoor revival meetings. At these meetings, he urged people to renew their faith in Christianity.

In Los Angeles, Aimee Semple McPherson, known as "Sister Aimee," built a great temple called the International Church of the Four-Square Gospel. Her Sunday services, broadcast live over her radio station, were theatrical events. They included an orchestra with 50 people, carefully staged lighting, and a dramatic entrance made by Sister Aimee. Her simple message of hope helped to restore the faith of thousands of migrants who were new to city life. She became so popular that reporters thanked her for creating work for so many journalists.

Many African Americans found inspiration and hope in the words of Jamaica-born Marcus Garvey. He launched a "back to Africa" movement, hoping his followers would create their own homeland and government. Until that homeland could be established, he called on blacks to

Marcus Garvey

build their own businesses and to develop pride in their African roots. Garvey's movement collapsed in 1925 when he was convicted of mail fraud for selling stocks for a business scheme. Although he was forced to return to Jamaica after his prison term, he had helped to inspire new confidence and pride among African Americans. As one woman said, "Garvey is giving my people backbones where they had only wishbones."

Peace in the Underworld

In May 1929, three months after the St. Valentine's Day Massacre, an organized crime meeting was held at a hotel in Atlantic City, New Jersey. The gathering, probably called by New York crime boss Frank Costello, included all the gang leaders from the East and Midwest, including notorious figures like "Lucky" Luciano,

The Ku Klux Klan reached the peak of its power in 1923 and 1924. The very size of the Klan made its acts of violence visible, although the vast majority of its members were peaceful. Many Americans were shocked, however, by the growing number of news reports telling of white-hooded Klansmen beating or killing their victims—people who were not white or Protestant. By 1925, support for the KKK was replaced by public outrage.

The center of Klan power had shifted from Georgia to Indiana, where David C. Stephenson held enormous power as the Grand Dragon. Stephenson was taking in $1 million a year, and he used it to spend freely and live lavishly. His way of life troubled the rural folk who made up most of the Klan membership. When he was arrested in 1925 in a case of kidnapping and murder, the scandal rocked the KKK's membership to the core.

Despite his political influence, Stephenson was found guilty of second-degree murder and sentenced to life imprisonment.

As a result of the Stephenson scandal and the violence, KKK membership dropped dramatically. By 1930, fewer than 10,000 members remained. The power of the Klan had evaporated. The organization was disbanded in 1944, only to re-emerge a third time during the civil rights movement of the 1960s.

"Dutch" Schultz, and of course, Al "Scarface" Capone. Johnny Torrio even came out of retirement to attend.

In response to the St. Valentine's Day Massacre, the crime bosses decided that the killings had gone too far. They drew up an agreement to establish the kind of organization Torrio had achieved in Chicago in the early 1920s. The gangs would pool some of their money for a more business-like approach to paying off politicians and police. Each gang was to have its own territory, which all the other gangs would respect. Any disputes that arose were to be handled peacefully by a commission headed by Torrio.

Satisfied with their accomplishments, the gang leaders headed home. Capone, who had just taken part in an exceptionally brutal murder of three former associates in Chicago, agreed to go into hiding for a few months. He planned to accomplish this by having himself arrested.

Chapter 6

FROM BOOM TO BUST
THE END OF THE JOYRIDE

*A*s the twenties drew to a close, the good times rolled on. Businesses continued to expand, and the stock market kept climbing. Every newspaper carried stories of ordinary individuals who invested in the stock market and made a small fortune almost overnight.

Millions of Americans assumed the prosperity was permanent. During the 1928 presidential election campaign, the Republican candidate, Herbert Hoover, declared, "Our American experiment in human welfare has yielded a degree of well-being unparalleled in all the world. [America] has come nearer to the abolition of poverty...than humanity has ever reached before."

By 1929, Hoover's words seemed cruel in their irony. The stock market had crashed, and a confused nation stumbled into the Great Depression. Hoover had miscalculated the future, and so did America's business leaders.

Capone Behind Bars

Al Capone also miscalculated when he planned to have himself arrested on his way home from the Atlantic City meeting of underworld kings. He and his bodyguard Frank Rio drove from Atlantic City to Philadelphia, where both men were arrested for carrying weapons. Such a charge usually did not lead to more than a few months in jail, which was what Capone wanted. Instead, the judge sentenced him to a full year. Capone had not counted on the anti-gang mood that was sweeping across the country. In response, law enforcers were cracking down on the underworld.

When he was finally back in Chicago, Capone made some changes in his operations. He was convinced that Prohibition would not last much longer, so he began exploring new operations. Since Chicago was planning a World's Fair for 1933, he thought it was a good time to organize members of some of the city's labor unions, including the truck drivers, chauffeurs, construction workers, and plumbers. Capone forced workers to join the unions that he supported and then siphoned off some of the union dues. He also opened some legal businesses, including dry cleaning, and he became a partner in a milk-distribution company.

While Capone was trying to conduct more of his work legally and above ground, the Internal Revenue Service (IRS) began investigating Capone's underground businesses. Capone had been careful not to leave a paper trail of his finances, but the IRS was determined to untangle his financial web. It wanted to bring him to court for income tax evasion. In addition to the IRS, Capone had to cope with a new team of Prohibition agents working in Chicago. Headed by a young man named Eliot Ness, these agents were far more persistent than others had been.

In 1929, a Chicago Prohibition agent named Eliott Ness developed a plan to destroy Al Capone's underworld operations and land him in jail. With the help of a small team of agents, Ness wanted to raid Capone's speakeasies and breweries and gather evidence against him. The nation's Prohibition Bureau agreed to Ness's plan, and he chose nine men to work closely with him. All of the agents were in their twenties, including Ness, who was 26 years old. This small, closely knit band was uninterested in any bribes offered by the gangs who kept Chicago supplied with alcohol. The newspapers nicknamed the young men the "Untouchables."

For the next two years, Ness and the Untouchables carried out raid after raid on Capone's operations. They often invited reporters and news photographers to accompany them, which insured that the raids would make news headlines. Ness and the Untouchables also managed to install wiretaps in several of Capone's establishments, including a nightclub that he occasionally used as his headquarters. The evidence that Ness and his men gath-

Eliott Ness

ered did not lead directly to Capone's arrest. But Ness did give the nation's Treasury Department some help in building a case against Capone for tax evasion.

Shortly before his death in 1957, Ness and a co-author wrote a book called *The Untouchables*, which described his campaign against Capone. The book became the basis for a popular, long-running television series, and it was also adapted as a movie, with Kevin Costner playing the role of Eliott Ness.

The Stock Market Crash

Throughout the 1920s, many people had great confidence in the nation's business leaders. These bankers and presidents of large companies were given credit for the nation's strong economic growth. While businesses were booming, more and more people invested in stocks. The upward trend of the stock market toward higher and higher prices for shares of stock seemed solid. Many investors began buying on margin. This was like buying a car on credit. The investor paid a small amount of money—the margin—and owed the rest to a stockbroker. The broker usually borrowed money from a bank to buy the shares for the investor. As long as confidence in the stock market remained high, the system worked. The investor would eventually sell his shares of stock at a higher price than he paid and make a profit.

Only a few saw trouble coming. On September 5, 1929, for example, an economist (someone who studies the economy) warned:

> Sooner or later a crash is coming, and it may be terrific. Factories will shut down...men will be thrown out of work...the vicious circle will get in full swing and the result will be a serious business depression.

On October 24, 1929, stock prices dropped sharply. People suddenly became uneasy, and their confidence in the economy was shaken. A group of bankers rushed to invest large sums, and the stock market prices rose again. But on the following Monday, prices took another plunge. By the next day—Tuesday, October 29—the bottom dropped out. It was a day that became known as Black Tuesday. As investors rushed to sell their shares of stock, they pushed prices down further. Investors lost

During the stock market crash in 1929, crowds filled the Wall Street area—the location of the New York City Stock Exchange.

money because they were selling stock shares at lower prices than they had originally paid. Stockbrokers, who were losing money, too, asked investors to repay their loans. But investors could not pay. On October 30, *The New York Times* reported: "Stock prices virtually collapsed yesterday, swept downward with gigantic losses in the most disastrous trading day in the stock market's history." Overnight, the business leaders and bankers who had inspired so much confidence seemed confused and helpless. In a matter of days, investors, banks, and business owners lost billions of dollars.

Hoover and the Depression

The 1929 stock market crash probably did not cause the Great Depression. Today most economists agree that a depression was unavoidable. The crash simply gave a mighty downward push to an economy that was already out of balance.

Although the prosperity of the 1920s was real enough, the economy was shakier than it appeared. Factories had been producing consumer goods at a frantic pace. But by the end of the decade, most of the people who could afford to buy cars, refrigerators, and other products, had already bought them. Industries were suffering from overproduction. Sales dropped and large surpluses of unsold goods were piling up. Consumers, and many businesses, were over-extended. They bought so much on credit that keeping up with their payments was becoming difficult. In addition, there were few regulations governing the nation's banks. The banks that had made unwise investments in the stock market were forced to close their doors. They did not have enough money for the customers who wanted to withdraw cash from their accounts.

Between 1929 and 1932, more than 86,000 businesses failed, including hundreds of banks. Every time a bank closed its doors, people lost the money in their accounts. Because the nation's economy was doing so badly, Americans who still had jobs saw their wages drop as much as 60 percent. In New York, for example, women office workers who had been earning forty-five dollars a week now took home only sixteen dollars. But at least they had jobs. By the time the economy hit bottom in 1933, over 13 million people were unemployed—roughly one third of the work force. There were no unemployment benefits in those days. Throughout the nation, people were lining up at soup kitchens, where they were given free food.

President Hoover assumed that those without money would receive help from their families or else turn to private charities. But the private charities, as well as local and state governments, were rapidly running out of money. Hoover insisted that the economic chaos was short term. When a group of citizens met with him in 1930 to urge him to use federal funds for public works, Hoover replied, "Gentlemen, you have come 60 days too late. The depression is over."

Hoover, and many others, were convinced that direct aid to needy people would make them dependent on government charity. He believed deeply in personal independence, or what he called "rugged individualism." He was unable to see that people's independent spirits were being crushed by the weight of despair.

Hungry men line up at a soup kitchen in Washington, D.C.

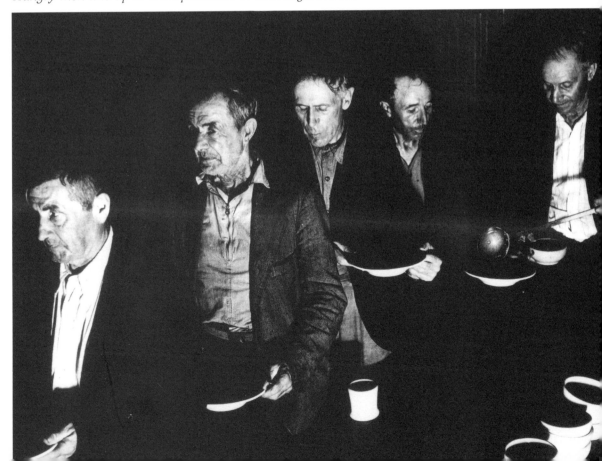

After World War I, Congress approved a bonus for war veterans to make up for the low pay they received during the conflict. The bonuses were to be paid in 1945. When the Depression led to unemployment for thousands of veterans, they and their supporters asked that the bonuses be paid right away. In 1932, a bill was introduced in Congress to release the bonus money.

To encourage Congress and President Herbert Hoover to approve the measure, thousands of veterans began a march to Washington, D.C.

This "Bonus Army" was made up of about 20,000 veterans, along with approximately 700 wives and children. They set up a shantytown (a small village of shacks) near the Capitol. The veterans were remarkably peaceful, maintaining order with military-style discipline.

In June 1932, the Bonus Bill was defeated in Congress. Most of the veterans stayed on, hoping to meet with Hoover or members of Congress. They were ignored and, in late July, police moved in to force them out. There was a fight, the police opened fire, and two veterans were killed. Hoover's response was to call out the U.S. Army.

General Douglas MacArthur led the soldiers in a vicious sweep through the shantytown. With swords, rifles, and tear gas, the troops forced the veterans to flee. Then the shacks were set on fire. Hoover's use of force against war veterans horrified Americans. One reporter commented, "By now, public hatred and contempt for Herbert Hoover has reached proportions possibly unique in the history of [our] Presidents."

The Bonus Army shantytown in Washington, D.C., was destroyed by U.S. soldiers.

In December 1931, the president finally proposed to give Americans help through the creation of the Reconstruction Finance Corporation (RFC). Approved by Congress a month later, the RFC loaned money to banks, railroads, and businesses with the hope that they would start rehiring workers and improve the economy. The RFC did save some banks and railroads from bankruptcy, but the effort was too little and too late to have a widespread effect.

Herbert Hoover ran for re-election in 1932. The Republicans believed that nominating anyone else would be an admission that their policies had failed. The Democrats nominated Franklin Delano Roosevelt, governor of New York. He was a man whose confident smile and forceful style seemed to promise action. "The country demands bold, persistent experimentation," Roosevelt told the voters. "Above all, try something." The voters agreed in overwhelming numbers. Roosevelt won in all but six states. Hoping that their new president's ideas and programs would provide relief, the nation entered a new era.

The IRS Gets Al Capone

When the Depression began, Al Capone displayed his usual generosity by opening Chicago's first soup kitchens. By late 1930, his three kitchens were feeding around 4,000 people a day. To many, Capone was still a kind of Robin Hood. But he, too, was about to face financial difficulties.

On June 5, 1931, Capone was informed that the IRS had enough evidence against him for a court trial. He was accused of attempting to "evade and defeat" the income tax laws for the period 1924 to 1928.

Like many underworld figures, Capone—and his lawyers— had assumed that illegal earnings were not taxable. A Supreme

Court decision in 1926 seemed to rule that they were taxable, but no one was sure. Two months before Capone was notified of his trial, his brother Ralph, and his second in command, Frank Nitti, were both convicted and sentenced to prison on similar charges. It was now clear that the government could indeed catch gangsters with the income tax laws.

Capone thought he was safe because he had never had any visible income. He owned no property in his own name and had never written a check. This presented the government agents with a tough problem. They had to find proof of some kind of income that could be tied directly to Capone.

Almost by accident, investigators found account books from the Hawthorne Smoke Shop—the front for some of Capone's gambling operations. The books showed that between 1924 and 1928, Capone had received for his share of the profits $1,038,660.84. This meant he had failed to pay an income tax of roughly $215,000. That income, of course, was little more than pocket money for Capone. And everyone knew that he was guilty of far more serious crimes, including dozens of murders. But here, finally, was some solid proof that could put the nation's most notorious gangster behind bars.

On October 18, 1931, Capone was found guilty of tax evasion. He was sent to the federal prison in Atlanta, the toughest in the nation. In 1934, he became one of the first prisoners at the newly constructed prison on Alcatraz, a rocky island in San Francisco Bay. In the past, Capone had enjoyed being a star prisoner, with a comfortably furnished cell and plenty of money to use where it would do the most good. Alcatraz was different. No one had privileges of any kind, not even a radio or a newspaper. Only family members could visit. The one-time Big Fellow suffered miserably. He completely lost control of his operations in Chicago and Cicero. About halfway through his

Capone leaves the Federal Building in Chicago at the end of the first day of his trial.

sentence, doctors discovered that he was suffering from advanced stages of syphilis, a serious and destructive disease that had first been diagnosed several years earlier.

After spending several months in the prison hospital, Capone was released on November 16, 1939. After more treatment in Baltimore, he returned to Florida with Mae and Sonny in the spring of 1940. Capone's empire was gone, although he still had enough money to live comfortably. His disease led to mental lapses, when he did not think clearly, and he shuffled when he walked. He spent his last days fishing or playing cards with the handful of friends who remained loyal to him.

On January 20, 1947, Andrew Volstead, the congressman who introduced the Prohibition enforcement bill in 1919, died at the age of 87. The next morning, by strange coincidence, Al Capone suffered a stroke (a break or clot in an artery in the brain). He died a few days later, just after his forty-eighth birthday.

Legacy of an Era

For many Americans, the twenties had been a wild and wonderful ride. It was also an era in which America became an urban, industrial nation, producing a wealth of goods that astonished the world. But these changes released massive economic forces that were beyond the control of individuals. The stock market crash and the Great Depression revealed just how powerful those forces were.

After the election of President Franklin D. Roosevelt in 1932, Americans began to realize that, in this modern age, there are times when the well-being of the nation's people requires governmental action. Herbert Hoover never saw the need for the government to act, but Roosevelt did. Throughout the 1930s, dozens of programs, costing billions of dollars, eased suffering and helped to restore hope. These relief programs came to be known as the "New Deal." Even these large-scale efforts were not enough to pull the nation completely out of the Depression, however. The economy didn't fully recover until World War II, when the demand for military supplies brought the nation back to full employment.

A New Crime Organization

During the years of the New Deal, the underworld developed a new style of organization. In most of the nation's major cities, gangsters formed tightly knit groups, often called "families." The most notorious of these were the Mafia families in New York, who maintained close connections with the Mafia "family" of Sicily, in Italy. The New York Mafia, and other crime families, tried to avoid leaving evidence that would enable the government to convict them on tax evasion charges. As gangland operations became more difficult to trace, Congress responded in 1970 with the Organized Crime Control Act. It gave authorities the power to arrest gang members on a variety of charges, known collectively as "racketeering." In 1987, the government used this law to convict eight men who were regarded as the leaders of the Mafia. Scores of lesser gang members have also been convicted of racketeering.

Perhaps the main difference between Al Capone's era and modern times is that gangland operations are no longer conducted as openly, and authorities frequently have trouble identifying the leaders. Occasionally, though, there is an echo of those earlier times. In 1972, for example, Joseph "Crazy Joe" Gallo was gunned down in a New York restaurant at his own birthday party. Except in movies and TV dramas, however, such bold violence is now quite rare.

Chronology

The Life of Al Capone

January 17, 1899	Alphonse Capone born in Brooklyn, New York.
1919	Al Capone joins Johnny Torrio in Chicago.
1920	Johnny Torrio takes control of "Big Jim" Colosimo's gang.
1923	Capone and Torrio move their headquarters to Cicero, Illinois.
1924	Capone interferes with Cicero mayoral election. Charles Dion "Deany" O'Banion murdered, touching off years of gang warfare.
1925	Torrio leaves Chicago—Cicero gangland empire to Capone.
1926	Gang attempt to kill Capone causes nationwide sensation.
February 14, 1929	"St. Valentine's Day Massacre" of seven Chicago gangsters shocks the nation.
May 1929	First meeting of all underworld leaders in Atlantic City, New Jersey, establishes territory for each gang. Al Capone arrested in Philadelphia for carrying a weapon; sentenced to one year in jail.
1931	Found guilty of income tax evasion; sentenced to 10 years of prison.
1932	Sent to federal prison in Atlanta.
1934	Transferred to Alcatraz, the new federal prison in San Francisco.
1939	Capone, suffering from advanced stages of syphilis, is released from prison.
January 24, 1947	Al Capone dies at age 48.

The Life of the Nation

1908	First Ford Model T produced.
1910	Protestant ministers publish *The Fundamentals* of basic Christian beliefs.
1914	World War I begins in Europe; United States remains neutral.
1915	Ku Klux Klan revived.
1917	United States enters World War I.

	Congress passes the Eighteenth (Prohibition) Amendment.
1918	World War I ends with Allied victory over Germany.
1919	Eighteenth Amendment ratified by the states.
	Volstead Act passed to enforce Prohibition.
	Labor strikes spread across the United States, raising fear of a Communist Revolution (the Red Scare).
1920	Nineteenth Amendment—giving women the right to vote—ratified by the states.
	Republican Warren G. Harding elected president.
	KDKA Pittsburgh becomes first radio station.
	For the first time, more Americans live in urban areas than in rural ones.
1923	Teapot Dome scandal exposed.
	Ku Klux Klan membership reaches an estimated 5 million.
August 2, 1923	President Harding dies; Calvin Coolidge becomes president.
1924	Coolidge easily wins presidential election; Robert La Follette's Progressive party gains 5 million votes.
1925	Scopes Trial in Tennessee challenges law against teaching evolutionary theory; both sides claim victory.
	Marcus Garvey convicted of mail fraud, ending "Back to Africa" movement.
	Ku Klux Klan leader David Stephenson arrested for kidnapping and murder, starting the collapse of the Klan.
1926	Gertrude Ederle becomes the first woman to swim the English Channel.
1927	*The Jazz Singer* becomes the first motion picture with sound.
May 20–21, 1927	Charles A. Lindbergh makes first solo nonstop flight from New York to Paris.
1928	Amelia Earhart, as crew member, is first woman to fly across Atlantic Ocean.
	Republican Herbert Hoover wins presidential election.
October 29, 1929	Stock market crashes.
1931	America is deep in the Great Depression; private charities and local governments cannot provide enough relief.
1932	Franklin D. Roosevelt defeats Hoover by a landslide in presidential election.
1933	Roosevelt launches New Deal as unemployment reaches 13 million.
	States ratify the Twenty-First Amendment, ending Prohibition.

Glossary

bathtub gin The name applied to all homemade liquor during Prohibition.

bootlegger Someone who makes, transports, or sells illegal beer, wine, or liquor.

Communist Someone who believes in communism, a way of organizing the country so that all businesses and property are owned by the country and profits are shared by all.

conveyor belt A moving belt in a factory that carries parts from one area to another.

conviction A declaration of guilt, based on available evidence.

cover A person, place, or thing used to hide a true identity or activity.

crystal set An early form of radio that amateurs could assemble themselves.

depression A time when many businesses fail, resulting in unemployment for some and lower wages for others.

economy The way business and finance is run.

Eighteenth Amendment The Prohibition Amendment, ratified in 1919, prohibiting the manufacture, sale, or transport of any alcoholic beverage with an alcohol content of more than 0.5 percent.

evolution The scientific theory, first proposed by Charles Darwin, that humans evolved from simpler life forms.

extortion The use of the threat of force to get someone to cooperate.

flappers The name applied to young middle-class women in the 1920s who dressed in a particular style and lived what they thought of as reckless lives.

front See **cover**.

fundamentalists Protestants who believe in the absolute truth of the Bible.

gangland The world of organized crime.

hijack To illegally take control of something, such as a car.

Imperial Wizard The title of the head of the Ku Klux Klan in the twenties.

Ku Klux Klan An organization that persecuted African Americans, Catholics, Jews, foreigners, and others who were not white American Protestants.

mah-jongg A Chinese board game played with tiles.

margin buying The practice of buying stocks by paying a small amount of money and borrowing the rest.

Model T The Ford automobile that became the first affordable and reliable car.

near-beer The only alcoholic drink that was legal during Prohibition. It contained 0.5 percent alcohol.

nickelodeons The first movie theaters, which operated in the early 1900s.

Nineteenth Amendment The amendment, ratified in 1920, that won women the right to vote; often called the woman suffrage amendment.

organized crime A group of people working together to plan and carry out illegal activities.

Red Scare The panicky fear of Communists. It led to a distrust of foreigners and other "outsiders."

sharecroppers Farm families who rented land to farm in exchange for a share of the crop.

sheiks Middle-class young men of the twenties who imitated the look of movie idol Rudolph Valentino.

speakeasy A private club that sold bootleg liquor and beer during the Prohibition Era.

stock Ownership of a part, or share, of a company.

stock market A place where people buy and sell stocks.

suffrage The right to vote.

temperance The word originally meant moderation in the use of alcohol, but by the 1850s, it came to mean the absence of any alcoholic drink.

woman suffrage Voting rights for women.

Source Notes

Chapter One

Page 9: "in this age of cities...temptations to our youth increase..." Ralph K. Andrist, ed. *The American Heritage History of the 1920s and 1930s.* New York: American Heritage Publishing Co., 1970, p. 28.

Page 13: "America's present need is not heroics..." Samuel Eliot Morison. *The Oxford History of the American People.* New York: Oxford University Press, 1965, p. 885.

Page 13: "Now for an era of clear thinking and clean living." Andrist, p. 45.

Page 16: "This service must be dignified." Ibid., p. 172–173.

Chapter Two

Page 20: "Mass production preceded mass consumption..." Marshall Davidson. *Life in America,* Vol. II. Boston: Houghton Mifflin Co., 1951, p. 284.

Page 22: "[Buy a Model T] in any color you choose so long as it's black." David C. King. *United States History.* Menlo Park, CA: Addison-Wesley, 1986, p. 492.

Page 22: "Good luck, Mr. Ford..." Ibid., p. 492.

Page 23: "The people who have made real fortunes check their brains..." Gertrude Mathews Shelby. "Florida Frenzy." *Harpers Monthly Magazine,* January 1926, p. 177.

Page 25: "Never before, here or anywhere else..." David C. King, p. 491.

Chapter Three

Page 28: "We were tired of Great Causes..." F. Scott Fitzgerald. *This Side of Paradise.* New York: Charles Scribner's Sons, 1920, p. 22.

Page 32: "Jazz has come to stay..." J.A. Rogers. "Jazz at Home." *Survey* (magazine), March 1, 1925, p. 665.

Page 32: "My candle burns at both ends..." Edna St. Vincent Millay. *Collected Poems.* New York: Harper & Row Publishers, 1921, p. 68.

Page 36: The "plain people...the Americans of the old pioneer stock." Dr. Hiram W. Evans. "The Klan's Fight for Americanism." *North American Review,* March–May, 1926, p. 33f.

Page 36: "Protestantism must be supreme..." Ibid.

Chapter Four

Page 41: "I've begged those fellows to put away their pistols…" Quoted in Robert J. Schoenberg. *Mr. Capone: The Real—and Complete—Story of Al Capone.* London: Robson Books, Ltd., 1992, p. 164.

Page 45: "the most astounding exhibition of tennis…" George E. Mowry. *The Twenties: Fords, Flappers, and Fanatics.* Englewood Cliffs, NJ: Prentice-Hall, Inc., 1965, pp. 82–83.

Page 45: "the greatest sports story in the world." Editors of *Life. This Fabulous Century, Vol. III, 1920–1930.* New York: Time-Life, 1969, p. 136.

Page 47: "We shouted ourselves hoarse…" Mowry, p. 82.

Page 48: "What's Al Capone done then?…" Schoenberg, p. 176.

Page 48: "My people thought Al Capone was Robin Hood." Schoenberg, p. 179.

Chapter Five

Page 49: "Oh hush thee..." John Mack Faragher, et al. *Out of the Many: A History of the American People.* Upper Saddle River, NJ: Prentice Hall, 1997, p. 758.

Page 52: "There are many reasons to believe…" Schoenberg, p. 229.

Page 55: "Garvey is giving my people backbones…" David C. King. *The United States and Its People.* Menlo Park, CA: Addison-Wesley, 1996, p. 548.

Chapter Six

Page 57: "Our American experiment in human welfare…" Herbert Hoover. *The New Day: Campaign Speeches of Herbert Hoover.* Palo Alto, CA: Stanford University Press, 1928, p. 176.

Page 60: "Sooner or later a crash is coming…" King, *The United States and Its People*, p. 561.

Page 61: "Stock prices virtually collapsed yesterday…" *The New York Times*, October 30, 1929, p. 1.

Page 63: "Gentlemen, you have come 60 days too late." Andrist, p. 181.

Page 64: "By now, public hatred and contempt for Herbert Hoover…" King, *The United States and Its People*, p. 569.

Page 65: "The country demands bold, persistent experimentation." Andrist, p. 231.

Further Reading

Altman, Linda Jacobs. *The Decade That Roared: America During Prohibition.* New York: Twenty-First Century Books, 1997.

Cohen, Daniel. *Prohibition: America Makes Alcohol Illegal.* (Spotlight on American History series). Brookfield, CT: Millbrook Press, 1995.

Collier, James Lincoln. *Jazz: An American Saga.* New York: Henry Holt & Company, 1997.

Cook, Fred J. *The Ku Klux Klan: America's Recurring Nightmare.* New York: Silver Burdett Press, 1989.

Denenberg, Barry. *An American Hero: The True Story of Charles A. Lindbergh.* New York: Scholastic Trade, 1996.

Feinberg, Barbara Silberdick. *Black Tuesday: The Stock Market Crash of 1929.* (Spotlight on American History series). Brookfield, CT: Millbrook Press, 1995.

Gilbert, Thomas W. *The Soaring Twenties: Babe Ruth and the Home-Run Decade.* Danbury, CT: Franklin Watts, 1996.

King, David C. *The Roaring Twenties.* Carlisle, MA: Discovery Enterprises, Ltd., 1997.

Stein, R. Conrad. *The Great Depression.* (Cornerstones of Freedom series). Danbury, CT: Children's Press, 1993.

Stein, R. Conrad. *The Roaring Twenties.* (Cornerstones of Freedom series). Danbury, CT: Children's Press, 1994.

Stockdale, Tom. *The Life and Times of Al Capone.* New York: Chelsea House, 1997.

Wood, Leigh Hope. *Amelia Earhart.* (Junior World Biographies series). New York: Chelsea House, 1996.

Web Sites

For more information and photographs of Alcatraz, go to:
http://www.nps.gov/alcatraz/

For more information on Al Capone, go to:
http://www.fbi.gov/famcases/capone.htm

To learn about the culture of the Roaring Twenties, including fashion, literature, and music, go to:
http://www.pandorasbox.com/flapper.html

To read about the main causes of the Great Depression, try:
http://www.escape.com/~paulg53/politics/great_depression.html

To view a movie about Temperance and Prohibition, visit:
http://www.cohums.ohio-state.edu/history/

For more information on Al Capone's partner, Johnny Torrio, go to:
http://user.mc.net/fig/mob/players/torrioj.htm

For photographs and more information on the St. Valentine's Day Massacre, go to:
http://www.MysteryNet.com/vdaymassacre/

To learn more about the stock market crash of 1929, go to:
http://www.lowrisk.com/crash/1929crash2.htm

To view photographs of the presidents and first ladies of Al Capone's period, go to:
http://lcweb2.loc.gov/ammen/phcoll.new.html

To view photographs related to woman suffrage, go to:
http://lcweb2.loc.gov/ammem/vtwhtml/vfwhome.html

For various curriculum links, go to:
http://badger.state.wi.us/agencies/dpi/www/WebEd.html

Index

Photo Credits

Cover and pages 8, 16, 30, 38, 43, 51, 59, and 67: ©Corbis-Bettmann/UPI; pages 4, 19, 21, 27, 35, and 55: ©Corbis-Bettmann; pages 10 and 26: ©Culver Pictures, Inc.; pages 11, 31, 33, 45, and 64: ©Library of Congress; pages 15, 61, and 63: ©National Archives; pages 25 and 46: ©Blackbirch Press, Inc.; page 40: ©Corbis; page 44: ©National Baseball Library.